Original title:
Roots in the Shadows

Copyright © 2025 Creative Arts Management OÜ
All rights reserved.

Author: Jude Lancaster
ISBN HARDBACK: 978-1-80581-903-5
ISBN PAPERBACK: 978-1-80581-430-6
ISBN EBOOK: 978-1-80581-903-5

Whispers of the Unseen

In the garden, the gnomes conspire,
They gossip and squabble, fueling their fire.
With shovels and hats, they plot from below,
As squirrels roll their eyes at the neighbor's show.

A worm wears a tie, feeling quite grand,
While crickets recite poems, so poorly planned.
The mole thinks he's king, but he's stuck in his hole,
As laughter erupts from a gopher patrol.

The Depths Beneath the Canopy

The mushrooms throw parties, oh what a sight,
With toadstools and wild tales stretching all night.
The raccoons bring snacks, a delightful surprise,
While fireflies dance, lighting up the skies.

A turtle laps lemonade, feeling quite spry,
While shadows play tricks, oh me, oh my!
The owls hoot complaints, they've lost their cool,
As critters below break every old rule.

Secrets Beneath the Thicket

The hedgehogs hold secrets in spike-covered dreams,
While bunnies share laughter over sweet berry creams.
A fox tells tall tales of glory and fame,
While crickets all cheer, they're wild and untame.

In the thicket, they dance, doing the twist,
While trees shake their branches, a sight not to miss.
A badger with style struts down the lane,
While everyone giggles, it's all just a game.

Echoes of Forgotten Earth

Dirt devils spin tales of ancient delight,
While worms moonwalk under the soft, silver light.
The ants throw confetti, it's their special day,
As dust bunnies cheer for their new friend, the stray.

A raccoon steals socks, claiming it's fate,
While beetles debate who could dance the best rate.
In the shadows, friends mingle, and secrets unfold,
As laughter erupts in this world made of bold.

Shadows in a Quiet Meadow

In the meadow where laughter plays,
Silly shadows dance in a maze.
Bouncing bunnies, a wiggle here,
Tripping over their fluff, oh dear!

The daisies giggle, the lilies grin,
While butterflies flutter, a whimsical spin.
A toad, wearing glasses, is reading a book,
But flips the page with a curious look.

Unspoken Links of the Deep

In the pond where fish dress up,
Wearing hats and sipping from a cup.
A catfish tells jokes, oh my, how they jest,
While the turtles roll back, they just need a rest.

The reeds whisper secrets, they giggle so light,
As frogs crack some puns under the moonlight.
But who's listening close? A sneaky old snail,
He'll tell you a tale, but it might not be pale!

The Subtle Weave of Time

In the fabric of laughter, stitches fall,
Each tick-tock brings giggles, that's the call.
The hours wear costumes, wacky and bright,
While minutes play hide-and-seek at twilight.

A grandma clock winks, it's no ordinary deal,
It conjures up dreams with a whimsical feel.
Time dances in feathery, wonky shoes,
While juggling dates; choose which one to use!

Threads of Forgotten Gardens

In the garden where mischief blooms,
Weeds tell stories, shaking off glooms.
A hungry gnome munches on pie,
While the roses plot how to dance in the sky.

The sunflowers nod, with petals that twirl,
As worms recite poems in a squeaky whirl.
Butterflies whisper of adventures they've had,
Even spiders claim they made each web glad!

Hidden Hollows of Renewal

In the garden of nowhere, weeds dance for fun,
An old snail winks, says he's never on the run.
Barefoot kids chase shadows, with giggles galore,
A lost shoe's a treasure, who needs one more?

Worms hold a meeting, debate on their luck,
While bats barter secrets; oh, what a muck!
The moon makes a cameo, dressed up in lace,
While crickets play tag, in a wide open space.

The Umbral Narrative of Time

A squirrel in a top hat, he tells quite the tale,
Of acorns and mischief, moments that fail.
The shadows do shuffle, each one with a grin,
As wiggly worms wiggle, their stories begin.

A clock on the wall laughs, counting down days,
While sunlight pirouettes in a whimsical craze.
Time's more of a jester, swaying like a leaf,
Whispering sweet secrets, oh, what a belief!

Whispers Beneath the Surface

Down by the river, the fish start to jest,
With bubbles of laughter, they're surely the best.
A frog croaks a joke, the turtles all snicker,
As a dragonfly twirls, oh, that slick little flicker.

Underneath the green, whispers rise and fall,
As ants form a chorus, a march or a brawl.
They thrive under leaves, in a world all their own,
Making mischief and memories, their grass-covered throne.

Echoes of the Unseen

Behind every thump, there's a mystery neat,
A raccoon steals bananas, oh, what a feat!
With giggles of ghosts that lead lives quite absurd,
They whisper to shadows, laughing without word.

The barn door creaks open, a poltergeist joke,
While the barn cats roll, feeling ever so woke.
In corners of night, they plot their next schemes,
Living for moonlight and luminous dreams.

Threads Entwined Below

In the dark where critters play,
Sneaky gnomes weave tales all day.
Twisting vines and giggles rise,
While squirrels dance in grand disguise.

Beneath the leaves, a party brews,
With acorns flying, who needs shoes?
The mushrooms groan with laughter loud,
While ants form lines, an awkward crowd.

Beneath the Canopy

Underneath the leafy dome,
Funky fungi find their home.
The beetles boogie, moving quick,
While roots play tricks — it's quite the pick!

A raccoon struts with style so bold,
Claiming the dance floor, truth be told.
The shadows wink, the whispers blend,
In this wild world, the fun won't end.

Tales of the Undergrowth

In tangled tales where mischief brews,
A lizard laughs at old tree shoes.
Worms hold court, their stories grand,
While snails slide past, a slow bandstand.

The brambles chuckle at their plight,
As crickets chirp into the night.
A dance-off starts, insect bling,
Caterpillars twist — oh, the joy they bring!

Ancestral Whispers at Twilight

As night descends, the fireflies glow,
Old spirits dance — they steal the show.
With giggles and grins, they flit and fly,
Trading jokes beneath the sky.

An owl hoots, "What's the fuss?"
While shadows murmur, "What a plus!"
In this twilight, laughter reigns,
With silly stories — joy remains.

Unseen Bonds of Belonging

In the dark where secrets sleep,
A squirrel's stash makes silence creep.
The acorns laugh, they play their part,
While roots and worms keep secrets smart.

A family brawl beneath the ground,
Competing for space—oh, what a sound!
The mushrooms gossip, sprouting wide,
As whispers dance with roots inside.

Life in the Mud

Sloppy boots and muddy shoes,
Frogs wear crowns, there's no excuse.
The worms conspire, wiggle with glee,
As puddles play, a jubilee!

The insects tango, unaware of fate,
They throw a party; it's never late.
Beneath the muck, a world abounds,
Where laughter echoes and joy resounds.

Lies Below the Surface

The grass is greener, but who can tell?
A rumor spreads, it casts a spell.
The gophers giggle with a toothy grin,
As earthworms plot their next big win.

Secrets hidden but not for long,
A snail sings softly, but gets it wrong.
With truths that wiggle and tales that twist,
Life's a circus, but who can resist?

Murmurs from Beneath the Pines

The pines gossip in the soft night air,
Telling tales of who's to care.
Below them, critters play their tricks,
As shadows dance in sneaky flicks.

A raccoon judges with a clever wink,
While chipmunks scurry, faster than you think.
The roots conspire, they hold the laughs,
In this underground world, you see the gaffs.

Silent Stories of the Underground

In the depths where whispers play,
Funny tales drift and sway.
Vines gossip about the rain,
While mushrooms dance to soothe the pain.

Beneath the soil, secrets bloom,
Laughter echoes in the gloom.
Worms tell jokes in squiggly lines,
As they wiggle through the vines.

Roots throw puns like tiny darts,
Making friends with fungi arts.
The underground is quite the show,
With comedic acts that steal the flow.

Mice in hats, oh what a sight,
Spinning tales till morning light.
Each hollow laugh a way to cope,
In a world that's filled with hope.

Shadows of Ancestral Echoes

Echoes bounce in ways so sly,
Old tales with a wink and eye.
Grandpa's socks, mismatched and loud,
Stand with pride among the crowd.

Whispers of the ones who've passed,
Tickle the leaves, stories cast.
Cousins share a wink, a grin,
Daring shadows to join in.

The family tree is quite the sight,
With branches dancing through the night.
Great-aunt's wig flies in a breeze,
As they crack up, "Do as you please!"

In the backdrop, secrets stir,
As shadows twist and softly purr.
Ancestral tales, a funny stew,
Lurking laughter growing anew.

Depths of the Unacknowledged

Down below the world's bright face,
Funny folks have found their place.
Rats in coats, pretending grand,
Throwing parties, oh so planned!

The depths hold stories, quite absurd,
About the things we've never heard.
A gopher's joke, a rabbit's pun,
Beneath the soil, they have their fun.

In corners dark, where no one treads,
Whispers rise above our heads.
The muffled chuckles of unknown kin,
Funny enough to make you spin.

With pocket watches and funny hats,
Timely jokes are served on mats.
All unrecognized, they still play,
In the depths, it's a cabaret!

The Buried Storytellers

Beneath the ground, the buried meet,
With tales so wild, they can't be beat.
A squirrel writes with nutty flair,
While worms recite without a care.

A hedgehog spins a yarn so bold,
About grand feasts of yesterday's gold.
Pinecones laugh, tossed without warning,
As dusk approaches - what a morning!

The buried storytellers, quite the crew,
Share their antics, funny and new.
An owl hoots for an encore call,
While shadows laugh, big and small.

From underfoot, the murmur flows,
A whimsical world, where laughter grows.
Each tale a twist, a playful chase,
Unraveled in their cozy space.

Underneath the Cloak of Night

In the dark where whispers play,
Silly creatures come out to sway.
A raccoon with a hat made of cheese,
Chases fireflies, wild as you please.

Mice in tuxedos dance on a log,
While frogs in sunglasses brag like a dog.
The owl reads poetry, sounding profound,
But the punchline always gets lost, so it's frowned.

Beneath the moon, the mischief unfolds,
With secrets of the night often retold.
Chirping crickets join in for a joke,
While the skunk tries to avoid being smoke!

So if you slip into the night's embrace,
Expect a humor-filled, offbeat race.
Laughter echoes where shadows do creep,
In the realm of the funny, let's dive in deep.

Veins of the Ancient Grove

Beneath the bark, a rumor spreads,
Of ticklish roots and drowsy heads.
Squirrels debate with wise old trees,
Who's faster? The breeze or the buzzing bees?

A porcupine counts each falling leaf,
While the beetles steal moments, oh what a thief!
Fungi giggle in their mushroom hats,
As the world's a stage for shenanigans and chats.

In this grove, the ground has a grin,
Tickling toes wearing mud as the skin.
Laughter and leaves intertwine and twirl,
In this ancient place where fun starts to whirl.

So wander deep where the giggles run,
In the veins of laughter, this life can be fun.
With stories hidden in each shady nook,
You might just find what your heart really took.

Gnarled Memories of the Undergrowth

Amidst the brambles, tales abound,
Of clumsy rabbits tripping around.
There's a hedgehog who thinks it can fly,
But only really plops, oh my oh my!

The thorns hold whispers from days of old,
Where the fox wore a scarf that was quite bold.
Each twist and turn has something to say,
In the tangled adventures that roam and play.

The bushes cackle, leaves rustle with glee,
As ants hold a meeting under the tree.
Echoes of laughter fill every crease,
In this delight where worries cease.

So skip through the paths where the shadows mix,
Gnarled memories, oh what a fix!
Nature's a comedy, a show for the keen,
With every corner, a new funny scene.

Shadows of the Silent Soil

Beneath the earth, a party does brew,
With worms and moles, oh what a crew!
They joke about carrots, so crunchy and bright,
While dreaming of things that grow overnight.

A gopher, dressed in a stylish cape,
Claims it can dig faster than any ape.
While earthworms wriggle with giggles galore,
As they dance on the surface and squirm on the floor.

The whispers of roots have tales to share,
About how raccoons combed their lovely hair.
With compost confessions bubbling with cheer,
In the shadows where soil makes fun crystal clear.

So tiptoe gently on this fertile bed,
And listen close to the laughter ahead.
In the fun of the earth, let your joy uncoil,
For the shadows bring humor, oh how they toil!

Silent Kin Beneath the Soil

In the garden, whispers play,
Worms debate the sunlit day.
Rabbits laugh at moles' lost plans,
While insects dance with tousled fans.

Potatoes shy beneath the haze,
Talking roots in silly ways.
"Who knew dirt could hold such cheer?"
The carrots giggle, no one near.

The snails slide in with quite a score,
Telling tales of what's in store.
"A juicy worm, a morsel grand!"
While daisies roll their petals and stand.

Beneath the heavens, life is packed,
In shadows deep, a world intact.
Laughter echoes, soft and bright,
In the depths, all feels just right.

The Depths of Hidden Heritage

Beneath the dirt where secrets sway,
Old gophers chat in a cheeky way.
"Who needs gossip from above?"
They chuckle at the sky's blue glove.

A worm winks, with great delight,
"I dug a tunnel, what a sight!"
But moles just laugh and keep on snoozing,
While beetles dance, none are losing.

The treasures here, a bit obscure,
Pumpkin vines with humor pure.
"Let's invite the ants for tea!"
They plan grand feasts, so happily.

In hidden depths, where none can peek,
Laughter echoes, playful and sleek.
A family tucked in soil's embrace,
In the shadows, they find their space.

Life Beyond the Veil

In the dusk, when light is frail,
Critters gather beyond the sail.
"The moon's too bright for a game of peek!"
They nuzzle tight, ready to sneak.

Fireflies flicker, lighting the scene,
As beetles boast, all dressed in green.
"I'll be the shiniest, just you wait!"
They flock together, hearts elate.

The elder roots tell stories old,
Of corny jokes, a treasure untold.
"Did you hear 'bout the peach who danced?"
Laughter flows as bugs take a chance.

In the shadows, life's a blast,
Tickling tales from futures past.
With laughter swirling all around,
In the dark, joy's always found.

The Uncharted Below

Digging deep through earth's delight,
Worms play chess, left and right.
"King of the Underground," they say,
Making networks, come what may.

Tunnels twist like jokes unfurled,
Moles break out, into the world.
"Who hid the grass? It's gone from sight!"
As critters laugh, what a heist!

Creepy-crawlies have a ball,
Singing songs, both short and tall.
"Do you think we are absurd?"
They giggle hard, for no one's heard.

Adventures lurk where light won't shine,
The underground, a mystery divine.
In laughter lost, they dig and jive,
Together, they thrive, oh how they strive!

Unraveled by the Moonlight

The garden gnomes had a party,
Wearing hats that were quite hearty.
They danced with ants and bees,
Under moonlight's playful breeze.

A squirrel tried to take the stage,
But tripped and fell off the page.
The daisies shrugged with delight,
At their neighbor's clumsy plight.

With laughter echoing so bold,
The shadows shared stories untold.
While the night bloomed with cheer,
The critters sang without fear.

As dawn approached, they all fled,
Leaving behind their dreams unsaid.
The night's escapade now a tune,
Whispered secrets beneath the moon.

The Undiscovered Below

Beneath the floor, a treasure trove,
Full of socks lost when they rove.
A small mouse in a pirate hat,
Sails on crumbs, how about that?

Cartwheeling beetles join the bunch,
Complaining how they missed lunch.
A dance-off led by a wise old rat,
Challenging all to a funky spat.

Toilet paper rolls become city sights,
Where fireflies race on starry nights.
The gophers giggle from their burrowed hold,
While the echo of laughter turns into gold.

The clock strikes a new day's call,
As the party ends in a sprawl.
The floors now quiet, tales kept deep,
In the hidden world where secrets sleep.

Lurking Beneath the Bloom

Under blossoms, creatures conspire,
A floppy-eared rabbit, a tiny choir.
They croon to the worms in the dirt,
About how the day's vibes can't hurt.

A ladybug boasts of her spots,
While a snail blinks and ties some knots.
The daisies titter at the scene,
As the leaf-caterpillar wears denim sheen.

In the shadows, fun takes flight,
With a clumsy toad in the spotlight.
He trips on roots, but gets right up,
Sipping dew from a lily cup.

When dusk falls, they pack away,
All their laughs from the bright day.
Beneath the bloom, they swell with cheer,
Hiding their secrets till next year.

Sanctuary of the Silent

In the quiet nook of a scruffy vine,
Lurks a hoot owl sipping on brine.
With a wink and a twist of his head,
He whispers jokes to sleepy bread.

A hedgehog dressed in a polka dot suit,
Is critiquing the taste of a berry shoot.
He roars with laughter, but then he sneezes,
Sending the insects off with breezes.

The fireflies light up the dense gloom,
While raccoons craft hats made of broom.
A dance by the pond, it's quite absurd,
As frogs join in, with moves unheard.

When morning breaks, it ends in a hum,
With critters scattered, all but one bum.
The tales of the quiet stay alive,
In the sanctuary where shadows thrive.

Beneath the Veil of Twilight

In whispers soft, the night unfolds,
Where secrets dance and moonlight scolds.
A squirrel steals pie, oh, what a treat!
As shadows giggle, they skip on their feet.

The owls wear glasses to read the skies,
With mischief brewing in their wise old eyes.
The stars throw parties, twinkling bright,
While sleeping cats plot mischief in the night.

The wind tells tales of socks lost in trees,
And rabbits that gamble on the summer breeze.
With laughter echoing through the leaves' embrace,
Twilight chuckles, wrapping us in grace.

Tangles of Time Beneath the Surface

The clock goes backward, what a surprise,
With giggling geese, we laugh till we cry.
Old shoes are dancing in a dusty room,
While spiders weave socks from leftover gloom.

A cat in a bowtie, thinks he's a king,
His subjects are mice that can barely sing.
Tick-tock, tick-tock, the humor unfolds,
As stories of bedtime are slowly retold.

Beneath the floorboards, a party's afoot,
With snacks leftover from last year's loot.
The shadows hold mysteries, oh what a team,
Join in the laughter, it's all like a dream!

Hushed Histories in the Dark

In a closet of secrets, socks start to chat,
Tales of old laundry, and a rogue ol' cat.
With whispers of mischief, they plot their next scheme,
While dust bunnies giggle, caught up in a dream.

Ghosts in pajamas, so cozy and sweet,
Share stories of socks that danced on their feet.
The wind sways the curtains, like a spectral friend,
Laughing at all the things time can transcend.

A squirrel in the corner, sneaking a bite,
Of cookies forgotten, out of sheer delight.
Together they chuckle till dawn breaks the night,
In the hush of the dark, everything's bright.

The Hidden Tapestry of Life

Weaving together with threads made of glee,
A tapestry dances, quite wild and free.
The puppies are plotting to steal all the bones,
While kittens are knitting hats from old phones.

In fields full of daisies, the ants hold a race,
With chic little brooms, they clean up the place.
Toadstools are chairs for the mice's grand ball,
As frogs leap for joy, admiring it all.

Tangled up laughter, where shadows collide,
Creating a chaos they try to abide.
In this quirky life, with love intertwined,
Funny little stories are waiting to find.

Sanctuary of the Subtle

In the nook where whispers dwell,
Laughter's echo breaks the spell.
Dancing mice with tiny shoes,
Join the fun, they've not a clue!

Beneath a hat, a gnome ascends,
His tomato plant, he pretends.
A plot so grand, it's quite absurd,
With madcap schemes that seem unheard!

Jokes exchanged like secret seeds,
In this realm, there's no such needs.
A jester juggles garden hoes,
As sunflowers giggle, everyone knows!

Mice and gnomes in cozy chats,
Trading tales of fancy hats.
In shadows deep, their laughter flows,
A sanctuary where humor glows.

Beneath the Canopy of Secrets

Under leaves of emerald bright,
A squirrel's dance is quite the sight.
With acorns stashed in hats so tall,
He spins around, forgets them all!

Beneath boughs thick and woven tight,
A caterpillar's wiggle-light.
He claims to know where treasure's found,
Yet trips on roots that twirl around!

The owl hoots jokes, it's quite a scene,
As bugs in bowties laugh and preen.
In shadows cast by branches wide,
The comedy troupe takes a slide!

Through segments of green, their humor spreads,
With whispers tangled in leafy threads.
Each chuckle rings, a soft reprise,
As moonlit giggles fill the skies!

Hidden Histories

In muddy patches, stories grow,
Of ancient plants and seeds we sow.
With every turn of the spade, we find,
A sprightly tale that's unconfined!

The potato sings in rhythmic glee,
While carrots boast of ancestry.
As onions cry, they share their fears,
Of salad dressings through the years!

A parsnip prances with regal flare,
Claiming lands beneath the chair.
With leafy crowns, they jest and jibe,
These hidden roots, a jolly tribe!

In shadows old, their laughter weaves,
A tapestry beneath the eaves.
With every plot, a joke unfurls,
In the garden of giggles, life whirls!

Veins of the Earth

Beneath the soil, where secrets dwell,
Worms spin tales that it's hard to tell.
With tiny hats and grins so wide,
They dig up myths that they can't hide!

A daisy dreams of grand ballet,
While clovers giggle their day away.
Beneath the surface, a funny strife,
As roots embrace the humor of life!

Moles are masters of underground glee,
With shovels made from jolly debris.
They host a dance beneath the ground,
Where laughter, like water, knows no bound!

So join the fun, and dig with grace,
In the hidden grooves of this lively place.
For beneath the surface, joy takes flight,
In the veins of the earth, all feels right!

Silent Growth in the Gloom

In the dark where whispers cheer,
Plants grow tall, without a fear.
They sneak a peek at the sun's rays,
Sipping light in sneaky ways.

Worms do the tango, all around,
As roots wiggle without a sound.
Fungi throw a mushroom bash,
Underfoot, they have a stash.

No one knows the plans they've spun,
While the world thinks here, it's done.
So hold your giggles, don't you dare,
Secret life beneath the layer.

Below the Surface of Understanding

Dig a hole, what do you find?
A party of roots, oh so aligned!
They send out signals, just to tease,
Making friends with the buzzing bees.

Underneath, they tickle the soil,
Gathering gossip, oh what a toil!
In invisible vines, they connect,
Where none can see, it's quite the spectacle!

Caterpillars shimmy, doing their dance,
While the ferns pull off a leafy prance.
If you listen close, hear a laugh,
At the party of the undershaft.

Ties of the Understory

In the thicket, bonds get tight,
Twisted friendships in the night.
Broccoli heads join the affair,
Sharing secrets with leafy air.

Vines tangle, but never fall,
Swinging, laughing, having a ball.
Rabbits hop and join in too,
In a madcap crew just for the view.

Roots gossip 'bout the rain above,
With squishy fungi, friends, and love.
The undertone giggles and chimes,
Making silly rhymes on the boughs of thyme.

The Unseen Connection

Feeling lonely, tree and shrub?
Below the surface, a cozy hub.
Buddies chatter in silent code,
Comedians on the leafy road.

Creepy crawlies join in the chat,
Sharing jokes, just like that!
With roots entwined, a tangled jest,
Together they shine, they're simply the best!

When the wind howls and the branches sway,
They hold their ground, come what may.
In the depths where no one goes,
Laughter erupts, as mischief flows.

The Secret Language of the Undergrowth

Beneath the leaves, a whisper brews,
Critters gossip in silly hues.
A mushroom winks, a vine sings loud,
As ants all march, they'd start a crowd.

Squirrels plot a nutty heist,
While crickets joke, oh, isn't life nice?
The thorns giggle with a prickly tone,
And beetles dance like they've found a throne.

Echoes from the Subterranean Realm

Down below, the snails hold court,
In their slow dance, they make retorts.
Rats trade tales of treasure found,
While moles pretend they're underground clowns.

Fungi giggle like it's a show,
As worms recite rhymes, just for the flow.
They toss around the dirt with flair,
And if you listen, you'll catch their air.

Tales of the Ensnared Anew

Caught in twine, the weeds conspire,
To trap a gnome or spark a fire.
The frogs croak jokes, oh, what a scene,
While spiders weave a spooky screen.

A mouse in a hat steals the show,
As the grasshoppers laugh, 'Oh, don't be slow!'
In tangled paths, the fun unfurls,
While dandelions face the world with curls.

Under the Gaze of the Silent Giants

Trees with arms crossed, like they know,
Watch the mischief of critters below.
Bugs play hide-and-seek in the bark,
While shadows dance till the skies go dark.

A squirrel juggles acorns with speed,
As whispers trickle like a mischievous seed.
Through the branches, silliness flows,
Where every breath is laughter that grows.

Beneath the Flicker of Stars

In the garden of giggles, we hide,
Where the moon becomes our silly guide.
Jokes sprout like weeds, oh what a sight,
Laughter blooms in the soft, cool night.

Beneath twinkling lights, we trip and fall,
Stumbling through shadows, we give it our all.
A dance with the darkness, we laugh and spin,
For what's life without a little grin?

The owls think we're nuts, the crickets agree,
But we radiate joy like a wild, crazy spree.
With shadows our pals, we swing and sway,
Playing hide and seek till the break of day.

Under the glow, mischief's our craft,
Silly antics and giggles shared in a raft.
We'll mess up the night with our quirky parade,
In the garden of laughter, where friends never fade.

A Cradle of Hidden Narratives

In the attic of secrets, we tell our tales,
Of socks without mates and forgotten snails.
Adventures in laundry and socks gone rogue,
Who knew a fabric could hold such a vogue?

The shadows whisper stories, all quite absurd,
Like the cat with a hat who thought he was heard.
Among dust bunnies, we're rolling on the floor,
Every tale more ridiculous than the one before.

A treasure chest of laughter stashed up high,
Silly memories painted across the sky.
The more we reminisce, the more it seems,
Life is just one big collection of memes.

So gather your giggles and brush off the dust,
From silly old stories, we gather our thrust.
In the cradle of yarns, we all play our part,
For humor's the rhythm that dances in the heart.

From Darkness, We Emerge

Out from the dark with a skip and a bounce,
In pajamas that sparkle, we start to denounce.
The shadows can't catch us, we're quick on our feet,
With jests flying high, we can't face defeat.

Tripping on laughter and errant socks,
Chasing our dreams like runaway clocks.
The night turns to day in a giggly rush,
As we plot our escape, making quite a fuss.

From closets and corners, we spring like a frog,
With goofy expressions leaving a smog.
We leap into daylight with mischief in view,
With friends at our side, there's nothing we can't do.

So here's to the night, we'll celebrate right,
For emerging from darkness brings forth the light.
With silly coconuts and socks full of cheer,
Each moment of laughter, we hold oh so dear.

Whispers of the Undergrowth

In the thicket of giggles, whispers abound,
With the rustle of leaves, we dance round and round.
The musty old shoes, the insects play tunes,
Unruly backyard antics beneath the cartoons.

With shadows for buddies, we sneak like a mouse,
Creating our jokes from the roots of the house.
Laughter erupts from the bushes we call,
Where we spin silly tales and giggling squalls.

Silly squirrels chuckle, the rabbits just gawk,
As we tumble through thickets, we giggle and squawk.
In gardens of nonsense, we proudly partake,
With fruit salad dreams and a chocolate cake.

The whispers of laughter, they linger and weave,
In the fabric of nighttime, oh what a reprieve!
For beneath every leaf, every twig, every clover,
Our secrets and chuckles will never grow over.

Veins of the Forgotten

In a garden of socks and old shoes,
Worms dance tango while I snooze.
Who knew that weeds could wear a crown?
Cabbages giggle, and we all drown.

Underneath the soil's thick guise,
Lies a party of ants with wild ties.
They gossip of carrots' latest news,
While radishes brag about their views.

The glow of mushrooms lights the way,
To gnomes who sing their hearts away.
Invisible laughter fills the air,
As trowels trot; they just don't care.

So, join the fiesta of the grime,
Where humor's engraved, and dirt's prime.
In a world where compost reigns supreme,
Even roots can live the dream.

Hidden Tapestry of Time

Under the stairs lies a forgotten chest,
Full of whispers and things that rest.
Chickens in coats and a rabbit in boots,
Sharing their secrets in feathered suits.

Dust bunnies joining the gossip parade,
Plotting a world where socks will invade.
A cat in a crown rides a lazy cloud,
While turtles waltz in a vegetative crowd.

It's a maze of laughter wrapped up tight,
With jokes planted deep, oh what a sight!
Time's elastic - it stretches so wide,
Surprises await in this whimsical ride.

Raccoons play poker, and squirrels bring snacks,
While shadows tell tales of wayward hacks.
An unseen thread connects all the dots,
In a game of hide and seek, who laughs the most?

Luminescence Underneath

In the dark where the funny things hide,
A disco of critters dance, full of pride.
Fireflies wear shades; they think they're so cool,
As shadows skip rope around a giant stool.

Sassy mushrooms, all dressed up for the night,
Sparkle and twinkle like stars shining bright.
With jokes that can cause the lilies to blush,
The giggles erupt - oh, what a rush!

There's a party in dirt, no need for a plan,
Where snails beat-box and their groove has a fan.
A hedgehog DJ spins tracks, wild and sweet,
And all of the beetles can't help but tap their feet.

So come take a peek at the glow down below,
Where the wittiest creatures put on a show.
In the depths of the soil, life's full of surprises,
With laughter that sparkles, all shapes and sizes.

Secrets of the Burrowed Deep

In a hole where the giggles dig deep,
Lie tales of hedgehogs attempting to leap.
A family of moles revamps their old den,
With a disco ball made of tin cans and pen.

Chickens wear hats, call themselves 'the elite',
While the roots, in a feud, argue who's sweet.
A squirrel named Doug devises a scheme,
While shadows unite for the grandest of dreams.

Pill bugs roll dice, hoping to win,
As worms tap dance with a cheeky grin.
Each whisper in soil, full of jest,
Beneath the surface, it's truly the best.

So discover the laughter that's hidden away,
In secretive tunnels where sunbeams don't play.
The mirth of the underground, oh what a delight,
Where shadows bloom in the heart of the night.

Echoes Lost to Time

In a garden where gnomes stand still,
Whispers of secrets follow the thrill.
The ghosts of lost socks claim their right,
Dancing with dust bunnies, what a sight!

Underneath eaves, the fairies grin,
Poking fun at the neighbors' tin.
Each creak of the floor tells a tale,
Of mismatched shoes and a ship that won't sail.

Old chairs remember every 'oops'
Of hurried lunches and spilled soup slurps.
With a wink, the shadows chuckle loud,
As they peek out from beneath the shroud.

In the attic, the laughter ignites,
As memories frolic in wild flights.
So raise a glass to the past unknown,
For every old thing has a story of its own.

Breath of the Earth

In the garden where weeds play hide and seek,
A worm cracks jokes, oh so unique!
The daisies nod to the ants in a row,
While a beetle steals the show with its glow!

Rabbits wear top hats, oh what a sight,
Sipping tea with the stars at night.
They gossip of vegetables, carrots so bright,
Completely ignoring the beet that took flight.

Underneath the ground, burrows confer,
Mice with monocles are quite the slur.
They strategize snacks from the pantry's stash,
While badgers debate on who's got the best mustache.

So breathe in deep, take in the fun,
Nature's a comedian second to none.
Laughter echoes through roots entwined,
In a world where whimsy and earth are aligned.

Muffled Songs of the Forgotten

In the closet, old sweaters hold a groove,
As dust motes dance like they're trying to move.
Forgotten toys sing melodies rare,
Of battles fought with no one to care.

In the cellar, whispers sing off-key,
Old bottles clink like they're full of glee.
A missing sock joins in with a cheer,
As they all toast to the days of yesteryear.

Books pile high, telling tales in a hush,
While spiders make webs in a creative rush.
The clock chuckles at moments we've missed,
As echoes remind us, we can't persist.

So listen closely, let laughter unfold,
For the past has stories that never grow old.
Each muffled song a treasure to find,
In the corners of minds, forever entwined.

In the Embrace of Soil

In gardens deep, the worms throw a ball,
With radishes bobbing, oh they have a ball!
Carrots are dancing, much to their delight,
While the potatoes giggle, hidden from sight.

Under leaves, the laughter shakes the dirt,
As roots swap tales of their daily flirt.
The sweet smell of muck brings smiles galore,
As ladybugs swoon over flowers that soar.

In this earthy realm, mischief is a game,
With every new sprout, it's never the same.
A snail in a top hat rides on the breeze,
While grasshoppers serenade with ease.

So dig in deep, and cherish the jest,
For hugs from the soil are simply the best.
Each laugh shared in this loamy embrace,
Is a nod to the joy that time can't erase.

In the Stillness of Forgotten Fields

In fields where laughter used to bloom,
The weeds now hold a funny gloom.
A cow named Ed with a silly grin,
Thinks he's a horse, let the games begin!

Cabbages dance, they flip and twirl,
As ladybugs have a silly whirl.
The sun is shy, playing peek-a-boo,
While crickets join in with a tune or two.

A scarecrow dreams of being a star,
Wishing on night skies, oh so bizarre!
The mice wear hats, just for the show,
Cheese balls and giggles make quite the flow.

So next you see a grassy patch,
Remember the fun in nature's catch.
For in each laugh, and every cheer,
The spirits of yore will always be here.

Whispers from the Depths

Deep underground, the roots conspire,
A gopher's tale that you'll admire.
He pulls a prank on the earthworm crew,
"Hey, look! I found a treasure for you!"

Moles gather round with popcorn bags,
As worms roll eyes and call them brags.
The shadows giggle, all tucked away,
Planning mischief for the light of day.

Small beetles debate, "Who's the best dancer?"
While ants just laugh, "We're the true chancers!"
A fungal rave in the musty deep,
Where secrets are shared, and no one sleeps.

So if you hear whispers from below,
Know the fun is where the shadows grow.
For laughter and joy are found in the grime,
In the depths of the earth, lost in time.

Beneath the Moonlit Canopy

Underneath the trees so tall,
The owls throw a wild ball.
Squirrels cheer, "Here comes the moon!"
While raccoons dance to a funky tune.

Shadows play hide and seek with glee,
As fireflies twinkle, "Look at me!"
Branches sway in a jolly jig,
While frogs croak out a lively gig!

The moon winks down with a silvery sigh,
"Don't tell the sun, but I am sly!"
Balloons of air to treat the night,
As stars dip low to join the sight.

Their laughter echoes in the cool night air,
In a secret world where none would dare.
So let's raise a toast, beneath the trees,
To the wonderful, wild, whimsical breeze!

The Veiled Symphony of Growth

A symphony played by roots below,
Instruments whispering songs they know.
The carrots hum, the potatoes croon,
While turnips break out into a tune!

Little sprouts dream of the sky so blue,
"Will we be flowers, or beans in stew?"
With a giggle, the onions start to weep,
As the broccoli aims for a grand leap!

Fungi join in with a funky bass,
"Watch out world, we're taking our place!"
The tomatoes roll with a round of applause,
Offering salad and love without pause.

So here's to the dance of lives underground,
Where laughter and joy are always found.
In the tapestry woven of petals and grime,
What happens in shadows stands the test of time.

Between Light and Dark

In the corner, a sock's gone shy,
Hanging out, beneath the pie.
Beneath the couch, where dust bunnies frolic,
They have their tales, both wild and comic.

The cat just yawns, unimpressed,
With the stories that they've confessed.
Chasing shadows, they giggle and play,
While we wonder where we left the tray.

Old chairs creak, whispering secrets,
Of clumsy spills and coffee regrets.
Mischief brews in the twilight seams,
Where laughter dances in fragmented dreams.

A bottle cap rolls with a clink,
In this realm, there's no time to think.
We hide snacks 'neath the bed's great expanse,
Creating chaos, disguised as chance.

Hidden Chronicles of the Ground

Underneath, where stories lurk,
A sandwich lives, a real good perk.
Hidden treasures, nuts, and chips,
Awaiting adventurers' eager lips.

A parade of ants, dressed in style,
Marching in single file, across the aisle.
With crumbs in tow, it's quite the feat,
Their tiny banquet, a tasty treat.

Toadstools giggle, whispering low,
About the mishaps of lawnmower woe.
Garden gnomes chuckle in their nook,
As the grass grows tall and strict with a look.

So raise a glass to the unseen crew,
Who find the joy in what we screw.
Life's little mess, a perfect delight,
Makes every evening feel just right.

Voices from the Depths

From the cupboard, a can starts to croon,
Reciting recipes by the light of the moon.
Spices whisper secrets of taste,
As the peanut butter debates with haste.

The fridge hums a dandy tune,
While leftovers dream of a grand platoon.
Mustard giggles in its funky jar,
Gossiping about ketchup's latest spar.

Down in the cellar, the bottles exchange,
Tales of yearnings and long-winded range.
Wine loves to boast of its aging flair,
While the soda pops up with a bubbly stare.

Cans and jars, in their jolly parade,
Share the laughter of memories made.
So lend an ear to the pantry's song,
In their laughter, you can't go wrong.

The Hidden Heartbeat

Beneath the bed, a squeaky toy sighs,
As the night creeps in, and courage flies.
Pillows conspire, plotting their dreams,
Whispering secrets, or so it seems.

Shoes, left out, plot a daring escape,
Wishing for legs, in this boundless shape.
They dream of adventures through puddles and rain,
While quietly finding solace from blame.

Cushions giggle, enjoying the tease,
As socks play hide-and-seek with such ease.
The clock watches, with a clicking stare,
But the pillow fort breaks through all despair.

Listen close as the heartbeats play,
In the whimsical life of a mundane day.
Laughter lingers in the softest spaces,
Where darkness dances and light embraces.

Subterranean Legacies

Beneath the ground where moles delight,
The secrets hide, out of sight.
Worms carry tales with jiggle and squirm,
While gophers chuckle, their roots confirm.

In the dark, the fungi swirl,
Like a dance party for each little girl.
With laughter and whispers, the soil does sing,
Of odd adventures that dirtworms bring.

They gossip and giggle, as they stretch and wriggle,
Chasing the earth's old, mossy giggle.
Life's funny business below the ground,
Where mischief and magic can always be found.

So tiptoe lightly and don't cause a fuss,
For the underground crew is a bit nonplussed.
Keep their humor and antics a little concealed,
For in the soil's antics, joy is revealed.

The Quiet Pulse of the Earth

In whispers soft, the ground does sigh,
As roots tickle grasses, passing by.
A debugged joke in the silence grows,
While the daisies chuckle at all that they know.

A twig snaps loud, the critters peek,
At the unseen humor of the bold little creek.
Creepy-crawlers' laughter fills the air,
As mushrooms dance on a jester's dare.

The earth does pulse with a quiet cheer,
Where beetles tell stories that no one can hear.
With a wink and a nudge, they wiggle in glee,
Declaring, "We're alive, Come laugh with me!"

Beneath the surface, where shadows play,
The antics of nature brighten the day.
So join in the fun, don't fall asleep,
For in nature's heart, the giggles run deep.

Interwoven Histories

In tangled threads beneath our feet,
Gnarled tales of old, all twist and meet.
The earth's a weaver, skilled and sly,
Spinning yarns where wild roots lie.

A squirrel's scurry sends ripples wide,
As the soil chuckles, it's hard to hide.
Old trunks creak back with a giggly whine,
Sharing secrets from their prime.

Beneath the bark, where shadows groom,
Fluffy tales bloom in the deepest room.
The weathered wood tells a punchline or two,
While the brambles chuckle, "What's new with you?"

With nature's laughter spun carefully tight,
The past and present join in delight.
So when you wander, don't miss the clue,
In the giggly tapestry of this earthy brew.

A Network of Memory

Underfoot lies a world of charm,
Where giggling rootlets twist and swarm.
A network spins with a cheeky flair,
As daisies sip tea in whimsical pairs.

The leaf-litter rustles, a secretive chat,
With an acorn's quip, "Do you know that?"
With each little nibble, life's tales unfurl,
In the garden parade, where laughter swirls.

The tree whispers gossip, shady and sly,
Like, "Where did you see that old butterfly?"
Through pathways of memories, funny and bright,
The underlings giggle into the night.

So while you step softly, lend them an ear,
For the jests of the soil, you'll hold dear.
In a world rich with humor, just look below,
And join in the giggle of nature's show.

Clusters of Origin

In the soil where giggles dwell,
Tiny whispers weave a spell.
Wiggly worms dance in delight,
Joking with the bugs at night.

Beneath the grass, they throw a bash,
Holding secrets in a flash.
A party hat made from a leaf,
Sharing tales of funny grief.

The daisies laugh, the roots just grin,
With every tickle on their skin.
While ants parade in wiggly lines,
The tiniest ones start making signs.

So here we find their merry jest,
Life underground, a funny fest.
Where laughter bubbles in the dirt,
And happiness is never hurt.

Underground Reveries

Beneath the ground, where laughter peeks,
Mice trade jokes and giggle squeaks.
A worm sports shades, oh what a sight,
Claiming it's the coolness of night.

Rabbits stomp and tap their feet,
In rhythmic beats, they can't be beat.
With each little bounce and silly grin,
They find the joy nestled within.

Ladybugs play hide and seek,
In the shadows, it's quite unique.
Twirling leaves in their merry dance,
Inviting others to take a chance.

So in these realms, where sunlight's shy,
The humor flies and spirits fly.
A hidden world, so full of cheer,
Where laughter echoes, crystal clear.

The Unseen Embrace

Under the surface, funny things brew,
As tadpoles chuckle, it's true, it's true!
A beetle slips on mud with grace,
While the sunflowers roll in a chase.

Tickles from the roots above,
Make the flowers giggle, oh how they love!
With silly pranks that no one sees,
They frolic with the buzzing bees.

The dirt is thick with hearty jokes,
In a world where all things grope.
It's a festival of crazy fun,
Where shadows dance and brightness shun.

Amongst the bits of nature's lore,
Grows laughter that could fill a score.
In unseen arms, a warm embrace,
Where every dark corner finds its place.

Shadows that Nurture

Underneath where sunlight fades,
Giggles rise like playful parades.
Mushrooms wear laughter like a cloak,
Each one winks—a jovial joke.

Squirrels share tales from the trees,
While giggling roots sway in the breeze.
The ferns whisper secrets with glee,
As shadows dance, oh so carefree.

A cactus cracks a pun or two,
About pricks and pokes, just for you.
Beneath their spines, the laughter grows,
In whispers soft, and friendly throes.

So come and peek beneath the ground,
Where joy and laughter can be found.
In shades of humor, life is bright,
A world of chuckles wrapped in night.

Shadowed Threads of Existence

In corners dark, the laughter hides,
A sock escapes where mischief abides.
The broom's confused, it sweeps around,
Chasing dust bunnies that just won't be found.

Forgotten things, they peek and tease,
Like strange old hats or mismatched keys.
Whispers of giggles from curtains dense,
They're up to something, but it's all pretense.

Underneath the couch, the secrets dwell,
A sandwich lost, with a story to tell.
The vacuum roars, a beast on the prowl,
Tangled up chords make it start to growl.

Yet with each stumble, we trip and roll,
Finding the joy in chaotic stroll.
For life's a mess with threads that fray,
But what fun it is to play all day!

The Unseen Dance of Nature's Bequest

In the garden dark, weeds twist and twirl,
They dance in silence, giving it a whirl.
The carrots giggle under moonlight's gaze,
While cabbages plot their leafy malaise.

Butterflies argue with the buzzing bees,
Who steals the nectar with such clumsy ease.
The tomatoes blush in their ripening game,
While the lettuce shouts, "Don't forget my name!"

The shadows sway, the gnomes stand tall,
With fishing rods ready for a garden ball.
Frogs leap in rhythm, croaking a tune,
While fireflies blink to the light of the moon.

Nature laughs loud in a playful jest,
With critters and plants, it's all a fest.
So join the unseen, the fun never ends,
In this leafy ballroom, where chaos transcends!

Life's Curved Path Beneath

Life rolls along on its winding road,
Where stumbles and trips become the code.
A pebble here, a banana peel there,
Each twist of fate gives us a scare.

The trees wave branches, a friendly salute,
While squirrels debate who's the best acrobat to boot.
Sidewalk cracks laugh with a chuckle or two,
As we dodge life's pitfalls without a clue.

In shadows so sly, the humor flows,
From clumsy ballet to comedic prose.
We're juggling dreams with one hand tight,
In this circus of life, we dance through the night.

So as we meander this quirky terrain,
Let's share our laughs, dance off the pain.
For even in chaos, there's joy to be found,
In the curves of our path, we're all glory-bound!

The Cloaked Embrace of Birth

A bundle of giggles wrapped up tight,
Newly arrived, but ready to fight.
With jammies askew and hair like a mess,
This tiny being's here to impress.

The world looks grand through sleepy eyes,
As parents are wrapped in love's sweet surprise.
Nappies and drool are just part of the game,
Laughter erupts, as who can complain?

In the cozy nook, where shadows play,
Little fingers wiggle, in their own ballet.
Hiccups like snorts, oh what a delight,
Each squeak and squeal is pure, pure light.

Whispers of love in a soft, gentle hum,
Cozy and snug, oh where do they come from?
In this cloaked embrace, joys multiply,
As life starts to bubble, under a gleeful sky!

Ethereal Roots of Yesterday

In the garden of giggles, they grow,
Wiggly tendrils, putting on a show.
With roots that dance and branches that sway,
They whisper secrets of yesterday's play.

Funky fungi wearing hats so bright,
Sway to the rhythm of the moonlight.
Each leaf a laugh, each petal a pun,
These quirky plants have so much fun!

Gnomes in the corners join the cheer,
Tickling the stems, oh dear, oh dear!
They tell tales of when shadows would grow,
And the mischief of bugs that put on a show.

So when you wander through this wild plot,
Remember the smiles that can't be bought.
For hidden below, where laughter's afoot,
Are giggling roots in a zany shoot.

Lingering Shadows

In a patch where the giggles collide,
Shadows stretch long, but they don't hide.
They juggle the light with a silly twist,
A peek-a-boo game, like they can't be missed.

Who's that lurking with a silly face?
Just a light-hearted ghost lost in the race.
He trips on a vine, oh what a sight!
With a chuckle, he dances into the night.

Ghostly whispers start to hum,
While playful shadows go thrum-thrum-thrum.
They toss out jokes like autumn leaves,
Warding off worries, just what one needs.

So next time shadows seem heavy and long,
Tune in your ears for their vibrant song.
In each dark corner, laughter will bloom,
A festival of fun finds its room.

Ancestral Paths of the Night

Beneath the moon's glow, a parade of old,
Ancestors prance, and they're oh-so-bold!
With mischief in tow and decades of fun,
Their dance moves make history come undone.

They poke at the roots with their wiggly toes,
While swinging through branches where the laughter flows.
Tales of mishaps and peculiar quirks,
Echo through the night like whimsical jerks.

With lanterns aglow, they raise a toast,
To the silly things we should cherish most.
For every ghost has a story to tell,
Of cake on the bed and of slipping on gel.

So roam on these paths where the night brings glee,
And find the hilarity that glimmered in spree.
For those who came before, oh, what a riot!
In ancestral giggles, there's always a diet!

The Depths of Our Beginning

In the soil where the laughter still grows,
Lay the depths of beginnings, as everyone knows.
Tiny critters perform in a vast ballet,
Tickling the tendrils along the way.

With every prank, a treasure's unveiled,
While squirrels in hats declare they've prevailed.
The depths of their antics spark silly lore,
As roots shake with laughter, calling for more.

From dusk till dawn, the chorus rings loud,
Nature's own jesters attract quite the crowd.
It's a ruckus of joy that bubbles below,
Where the old tales of whimsy effortlessly flow.

So dig up the fun, let the giggling thrive,
In the dark of the night, our spirits come alive.
For in every beginning, a chuckle we trace,
In the depths of our history, we find our place.

Beneath the Space of Day

In a garden where daisies do prance,
The gnomes whisper secrets, take a chance.
Worms in top hats waltz through the blooms,
While beetles debate the latest cartoons.

Amidst the sun's rays, a squirrel does skip,
With acorns of gold, it hatches a trip.
The hedgehogs wear shades, sipping on tea,
It's a wild life fest, come join the spree!

Underneath the soil, there's laughter galore,
With critters at play, who could ask for more?
They dance in the dark, but not out of fright,
For shadows bring fun, even in the night!

So come grab a shovel, join the delight,
Where sunlight and shadows meet in a fight.
Each laugh in the dirt, a joy to behold,
In this quirky world, where the silly unfold.

Unveiling the Veil

A ghost in a tutu, now isn't that strange?
Twirls on the porch, oh, it loves to exchange!
With the cat who just stares, wide-eyed, quite unfazed,
While the moon plays the tune, they dance unamazed.

Behind every curtain, a story's at play,
Where shadows get sassy, and giggles decide sway.
The starlings all gossip, a raucous affair,
As the owls roll their eyes, giving blank stares of despair.

What lies in the corners, who knows what exists?
A sock with a smile, a sock puppet tryst!
They whisper of wishes, with laughter that hums,
Oh, the fun that awaits when the day softly succumbs!

So peek through the veil, see the silliness strife,
Where shadows are schooled in the art of good life.
Each giggle composes a grand twilight song,
In the wacky embrace where we all just belong.

The Forgotten Is All Around

An old shoe sits quietly, dust on the lace,
Whispers of adventures, a smile on its face.
It once ran with children, oh what a delight,
In its dreams, it still dances, through the long night.

The clocks tick their tales, but nobody hears,
Time's clumsy ballet, bringing chuckles and cheers.
A paperclip army, they march to the scrap,
Their leader, a thumbtack, makes sure there's a nap.

In the corners collect stories, the lost and the found,
With kitchen sponges dreaming, distinctly unbound.
The mice with their mischief, they twirl and they spin,
In the shadows of silence, the laughter begins.

So laugh at the objects that gather around,
Each tells a tale, if you look where they're found.
For the forgotten are lively, and life feels like play,
In the chaos of clutter, we find joy every day.

Life's Quiet Resilience

A wilting flower brightens with plot,
A joke in its petals, oh, what have we got?
It chuckles at storms, with a wink and a sigh,
As both sunshine and rain paint the pastel sky.

In the crevices deep, where the weeds like to fight,
The dandelions giggle, saying, "We're alright!"
Their laughter, a nuisance, a giddy delight,
Poking through sidewalks to share in the light.

The ants march in rhythm, a parade every day,
With breadcrumbs for hats, oh, they fashion their way.
Each trail tells a tale of resilience so grand,
Where humor's the anthem, and joy is the plan.

So here's to the quirks that make life a scene,
In shadows and sunshine, we're all in between.
With laughter and spirit, we stand side by side,
In this funny old garden, our hearts open wide.

www.ingramcontent.com/pod-product-compliance
Lightning Source LLC
Chambersburg PA
CBHW070312120526
44590CB00017B/2638